Inclined Planes

by Anne Welsbacher

Consultant:
Philip W. Hammer, Ph.D.
Assistant Manager of Education
American Institute of Physics

Bridgestone Books
an imprint of Capstone Press
Mankato, Minnesota

Bridgestone Books are published by Capstone Press
151 Good Counsel Drive, P.O. Box 669, Mankato, Minnesota 56002
http://www.capstone-press.com

Library of Congress Cataloging-in-Publication Data
Welsbacher, Anne, 1955–
    Inclined planes/by Anne Welsbacher.
    p. cm.—(The Bridgestone Science Library)
    Includes bibliographical references and index.
    Summary: Uses everyday examples to describe inclined planes as simple machines
that make lifting, pushing, moving, and building easier.
    ISBN 0-7368-0610-5
    1. Inclined planes—Juvenile literature. [1. Inclined planes.] I. Title. II. Series.
TJ147.W46 2001
621.8′11—dc21

                                                                    00-025773

Editorial Credits
Rebecca Glaser, editor; Linda Clavel, cover designer; Kia Bielke, illustrator; Katy Kudela,
    photo researcher

Photo Credits
David F. Clobes, 8, 12, 20
Index Stock Imagery, 18
Jack Glisson, 14
Photo Network/Dennis Junor, 16
Robert Maust/Photo Agora, 10
Unicorn Stock Photos/Jeff Greenberg, 4
Visuals Unlimited/Jeff Isaac Greenberg, cover

1 2 3 4 5 6 06 05 04 03 02 01

Table of Contents

Simple Machines

Simple machines make work easier or faster. Work is using force to move an object across a distance. Lifting, moving, pushing, and pulling are kinds of work. An inclined plane is a simple machine that makes work easier.

force
anything that changes the speed, direction, or motion of an object

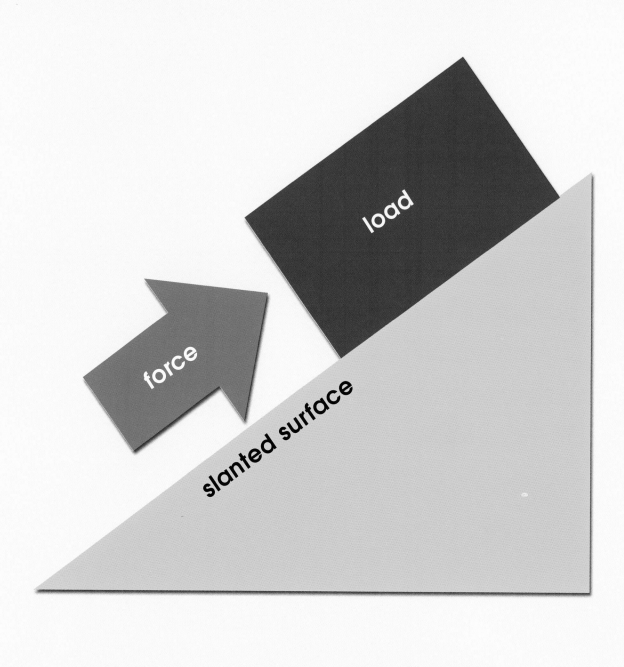

Parts of an Inclined Plane

An inclined plane is a surface that slants. You can use inclined planes to move a load up or down. Lifting a heavy load takes a lot of force. You need less force to push it up an inclined plane. But you have to move the object across a longer distance.

Using Inclined Planes to Lift

A ramp is an inclined plane. Moving something up a ramp is easier than lifting it straight up. People who use wheelchairs move from one level to another using ramps.

Using Inclined Planes to Move Up

Mountains are steep inclined planes. People cannot drive straight to the top of steep mountains. People build roads that wind around high mountains. The roads are gradual inclined planes. Cars travel a longer distance. But the gradual inclined plane makes the drive easier.

gradual

not steep; a gradual inclined plane gets higher over a long distance.

11

Using Inclined Planes to Move Down

The force of gravity pulls objects down inclined planes. Children move quickly down slides. Rainwater runs down a roof. The bottom of a bathtub is a gradual inclined plane. The water runs down the plane into the drain.

gravity
a force that pulls objects to Earth

inclined plane

cylinder

threads

The Smallest Inclined Planes

A screw is another simple machine. A screw is an inclined plane that winds around a cylinder. The inclined plane forms threads around the screw. The threads help screws move into wood.

cylinder
a tube-shaped object

Stairs and Ladders

Stairs and ladders are inclined planes. They help people move from one level to another. Stairs and ladders have steps. The steps help people move up or down more easily or more quickly.

Wedges

Wedges also are simple machines. An ax is a wedge made of two inclined planes back to back. An ax helps split logs. A doorstop is a wedge made of one inclined plane. A doorstop pushed under a door holds it open.

Inclined Planes in Other Machines

Simple machines can be part of complex machines. A gumball machine has many parts. It has screws, levers, and other parts. An inclined plane called a chute drops the gumball down.

complex
having many parts

Hands On: Slower or Faster?

This experiment compares gradual and steep inclined planes.

What You Need

Five thick books
A board or a shelf from a bookshelf
A toy car
A stopwatch or clock with a second hand
Paper and pencil
A friend

What You Do

1. Put one end of the board on one book. Place another book on the table next to the low end of the board.
2. One person puts the car at the high end of the board and lets go. The other person times how long the car takes to hit the book. Record the time on the piece of paper.
3. Put another book on top of the first one. Put the high end of the board on top of the two books.
4. Repeat step two. How long did the car take to hit the book this time?
5. Try the experiment again with three or four books.

Earth's gravity pulls objects down inclined planes. The steeper the inclined plane, the faster the car moves.

Words to Know

chute (SHOOT)—a narrow, tilted path for objects; a gumball drops down a chute from a gumball machine.

gravity (GRAV-uh-tee)—the force that pulls objects to Earth; gravity pulls objects down inclined planes.

ramp (RAMP)—a slanted surface that joins two levels

screw (SKROO)—an inclined plane wound around a cylinder; screws are simple machines used to lift, move, or join objects together.

wedge (WEDGE)—an object that has a wide end and a narrow end; wedges are used to cut or split apart objects.

Read More

Glover, David. *Ramps and Wedges.* Simple Machines. Crystal Lake, Ill.: Rigby Interactive Library, 1997.

Hodge, Deborah. *Simple Machines.* Starting with Science. Toronto: Kids Can Press, 1996.

Rush, Caroline. *Slopes.* Simple Science. Austin, Texas: Raintree Steck-Vaughn, 1997.

Internet Sites

Inventors Toolbox: Simple Machines
http://www.mos.org/sln/Leonardo/InventorsToolbox.html

School Zone, Simple Machines
http://www.science-tech.nmstc.ca/maindex.cfm?idx=1394&language=english&museum=sat&function=link&pidx=1394

Simple Machines
http://www.fi.edu/qa97/spotlight3/spotlight3.html

Index